i

PRAISE FOR *HOW TO SELF PUBLISH INEXPENSIVE BOOKS AND EBOOKS: U.S. EDITION*

"You have finished writing your book. After much consideration, you have decided to take the self-publishing route to see your book in the market and retain full control of the entire process all the way to the final game of marketing. It's a big job, but where do you start?

"First, you must have your book properly edited. Then you have to look at layout options and cover design. You have to consider cost. How much are you willing to pay for the end product? So many questions.

"Perhaps one of the biggest questions is whom to trust. Who in the self-publishing industry is not going to overcharge you and take advantage of you? Especially if it's your first book and you're at a loss as to where to start and how to go about the process.

"**Look no further. William Allan has written the book for you.**

"*How to Self Publish Inexpensive Books and Ebooks: U.S. Edition* is **a very thorough guide** which will walk you through the process carefully, step by step.

"From editing, to layout and cover design, to the actual decision of whom to trust, and then the final process of marketing and getting the book recognized by readers everywhere, **this author has answered all of your questions and more.** There are lists of trustworthy book and ebook printers and publishers . . . in the United States, including rough estimates of fees charged and links to their sites . . . There are also lists of sites that will review your book and the fees.

"**A very useful guide and a must-have** for anyone considering the self-publishing book and ebook process."

Five-star review by Emily-Jane Hills Orford for Readers' Favorite

How to Self Publish Inexpensive Books and Ebooks: U.S. Edition

WILLIAM ALLAN

Printed and Bound in the United States of America

Second Edition First Printing

Cover image: © Sergey Khakimullin / **Dreamstime.com**

Cover design by Tim Durning, Scribe Inc.

Page layout by Jamie Harrison, Scribe Inc.

ISBN: 978-1-4956-1864-2

Library of Congress Control Number: 2018901652

CONTENTS

INTRODUCTION

12 REASONS TO SELF PUBLISH YOUR BOOK

1. You don't want your book to take 18 to 24 months or more to be printed.
2. By self publishing, your book will be printed. No rejection letters. And a traditional publisher won't tell you they will print your book, and then never do so, ruining the author's career. This has actually happened to some authors.
3. You want to keep creative control over the production of your book.
4. You want to keep more of your royalties. Self-published authors earn higher royalty rates than those who use traditional publishing (the Big Five very large publishing houses).
5. A traditional publisher may give you an advance on royalties, but the publisher owns the rights to your book. If you self publish, you retain all the rights to your book.
6. You are determined to get your book out to readers because you think it will find an audience or you feel you have something to contribute to the literary scene.
7. If you self publish, you don't need a literary agent.
8. Traditional publishers won't take unsolicited manuscripts. So by self publishing, an agent won't hold your future dreams of publishing in his/her overworked hands.

9. Some self publishers employ ghostwriters, so you can submit an uncompleted manuscript.
10. The cost to self publish a book is lower today than you ever imagined (see Chapter 5). There is now no excuse. If you have a book inside you crying to get out, write it and self publish it.
11. Many self-published books have been very successful and independent authors have reaped the benefits.
12. Self publishing your book can be, without a doubt, a very viable option to success for an author.

So keep writing. Commit yourself to write the best books you can. And don't give up.

But who can you trust with your manuscript?

How do you choose a publisher?

If you are reading this, you have let *How to Self Publish Inexpensive Books and Ebooks: U.S. Edition* help you get your masterpiece out to readers.

Thank you.

WHY DID I WRITE THIS BOOK?

Many authors spend months or even years writing their first book only to be intimidated by the publishing and marketing of their new creation.

I worked for nearly 30 years in the newspaper business as a reporter then copy editor doing page makeup.

But I quickly learned after writing my first book that the printing of books was a lot more complicated than the printing of newspapers.

The journey to get my first book, *Four Murders in a Small Town*, published as a paperback and then an ebook taught me so much about the modern self-publishing industry. I thought I'd write this book in hopes of making it easier for some future U.S. first-time authors.

I was searching for the best price to produce my book. I, like many first-time authors, have lots of words but little money. I'm retired living on a fixed income.

There are many books telling you how to self publish your book for less than $100 or virtually free. They recommend you create your cover on CreateSpace or IngramSpark and let them publish your book. Some printers now even provide authors with information on how to layout the pages of their books.

You can do that, but you will get a book that will look like it was self published and not a professional product that will compete with books from traditional publishers.

You need professional editing, cover design and page layout.

Professional editing prevents your book from being printed with grammatical errors and spelling mistakes that instantly tell a reader they don't want to read your book.

Professional cover design will give you a cover that will make your book stand out from the cheaply done books and give your book a leg up in competing with the traditional books in your genre category.

Professional page layout will make the interior of your book look like it was produced by a traditional publishing house. You can ask for headers and footers on each page and other devices that will cause readers to want to read your book and look forward to every page.

I cite 35 U.S. book and/or ebook publishers in this book, most of them in Chapters 3 and 6. You can choose where to take your manuscript and who to trust with it while keeping your budget in mind.

Chapter 10 includes three publishers who offer extensive marketing and promotion of your book with every proposal they offer.

You can get your book published with professional cover design and page layout for as little as $245 (see Chapter 5).

The title of this book emphasizes it is aimed at finding inexpensive, quality book publishers for authors so they can market their book with confidence (see Chapter 9 for 25 ways to market your book). Those authors will know their book has a far better chance than most of finding an audience and being successful.

There are no guarantees in the book publishing industry today. I cannot and will not guarantee your book will sell thousands of copies and you will become a household name.

What I can guarantee, if you follow the ideas in this book, is you will enter the market with a book that has all the prerequisites for success. Whether it is successful depends on your marketing efforts and, truthfully, some luck.

But you will be preparing to market a book people will want to read rather than a book they will be sorry they purchased.

The 35 book and ebook publishers cited in this book range from one that will print your book in 48 hours (**48 Hour Books**) to several publishers who value their craft and employ professional layout, design and print specialists.

They also include publishers that will print your book and leave all the marketing to you and print-on-demand (POD) companies with large marketing departments.

One of the 35 (**Dorrance Publishing**) provides $1,000 in marketing assistance in every book proposal they issue (see Chapter 10). Another publisher mentioned in Chapter 10 (**Wheatmark Publishing**) has a good record of helping authors sell their books and go on to even greater success.

One publisher (**Entrada Publishing**), if they accept your book, will pay the costs of producing, printing, marketing and distribution of the book and pay the author royalties.

For those of you who have written a novel and want some assistance in finding an economical printer, I haven't forgotten you. I will deal with your specific situation and those costs in **Chapter 10**.

I also tell you which printer and publisher book packages offer author websites since, as I mention in **Chapter 9**, an author website is key to marketing a book.

And **Chapters 6** and **7** feature producers of ebooks, an option every author should consider given their inexpensive cost (see **Chapter 7**) and percentage of the book market.

Finally, I want to state that I have received no monetary compensation or any publishing service for any of the recommendations, opinions, book and ebook "winners" or options for novelists that I cite in this book.

In fact, two publishers refused to publish either the Canadian edition or this U.S. edition. They had their reasons (competing publishers or competing bookstores mentioned in the book or ebook).

But both companies are recommended in this book because the reasons cited were specific to this book and will not affect any other author.

And their services, I believe, may be of value to the readers of this book.

I wrote this book to help first-time authors and those seeking a new self publisher. I hope you enjoy reading this book. I hope it will be a learning experience. And if it helps you select an inexpensive publisher for your manuscript, congratulations!

WHAT COMMITMENT TO AUTHORS DO SOME PUBLISHERS HAVE?

I also tell you when any printer mentioned in this book does not have a toll-free telephone number.

While the cost of calling long distance is not excessive, I believe printers should both encourage and make it easy for authors to contact them.

Email is fine, but I have found you can spend days emailing a printer back and forth when a short phone conversation solves the problem in minutes.

Some big printers don't have a phone number at all.

I know it's in their business plans, but I think that is disconcerting. They just refuse to spend the money to hire and train some people to answer phones.

You wonder what their real commitment is to authors when they refuse to speak to them.

CHAPTER

1

The Basics

First the basics.
How to organize the pre-story pages of your book.

COPYRIGHT PAGE

After the title page comes the copyright page.
It should be organized as follows:

Copyright © 2018 by (your name)
All rights reserved. No part of this book may be reproduced in any manner without permission except in the case of brief quotations included in critical articles and reviews. For more information, please contact the author.
Printed and Bound in the United States of America at (your publisher's company name).
For fiction works only: All characters appearing in this work are fictitious. Any resemblance to persons, living or dead, is purely coincidental.

International Standard Book Number (ISBN)
Necessary for selling your book in retail stores. An ISBN number is needed for a softcover, hardcover and each ebook format.

Bowker sells ISBNs in the U.S. If you supply your own ISBNs to your publisher, you will become the publisher of your book.

Bowker charges $125 for one ISBN and $295 for 10 ISBNs. You can get one ISBN and one barcode for $150 or 10 ISBNs and one barcode for $320.

https://www.myidentifiers.com

You will pay for ISBN numbers from your publisher if you get your book printed in the U.S., unless you purchase a package in which case it will often be included.

Using a publisher-supplied ISBN makes them the publisher of your book. Some publishers, like BookBaby, insist on being the publisher of your book even if you supply your own ISBN because they say they must be the publisher so distributors know who to order the book from.

That's not a problem, generally. All my books used publisher-supplied ISBNs. But if you have a question about how Amazon is listing your book, Amazon won't answer your question. They will insist you get your publisher to ask them the question and get the answer, assuming Amazon will even give them an answer.

Edition and Printing History

First Edition First Printing.

Credits

Cover illustration by (credit for cover illustrator, if used).

Cover image © (credit for cover image or images if used, get permission to use each image).

Page layout by (name of employee at your printer or the company).

Cover design by (name of employee at your printer or the company).

Author photo by (name of author's photographer).

Library of Congress Control Number

Helps libraries and bookstores access correct cataloguing data. Your U.S. publisher can supply this or apply for it. An author cannot apply. Must be obtained before publication. Go to **www.loc.gov** and search lccn.

Cataloging in Publication (CIP)

CIP is for books that will likely be stocked by libraries. They use it for cataloging purposes. Self-published books are not eligible in the U.S. Ask your publisher if your book is eligible for CIP. Publishers generally apply rather than authors. CIP is for books prior to publication. Published books are not eligible.

Copies and other books

Additional copies of this book can be ordered at (enter website).

Other works by this author (list them and where they can be purchased).

Should you register your copyright?

It's not required but registering can be useful in the event of a legal dispute over copyright infringement.

In the United States, registration costs $55. Information and registration can be obtained at **www.copyright.gov**

OTHER PRE-STORY PAGES

I highly recommend *4 Ways to Perfectly Preface Your Book* on the Friesen Press blog at **www.friesenpress.com**
Here's a short summary:

Foreword is written by someone other than the author. It introduces the author. A peer vouching for your expertise is a great asset. Forewords are usually in nonfiction books.

Preface is written by the author or editor. It imparts nonessential information about your book to the reader.

Introduction is usually only in nonfiction books. It allows the author to provide information on the book which shows him or her to be an expert on the subject.

Prologue is only in fiction books. It presents the reader with an important moment from the story. Usually also accompanies an Epilogue at the end of the book.

Acknowledgments

This is the place to thank people who were crucial in your book coming to life. The production people were thanked on the copyright page. This is the place to thank other people who played a pivotal role in the writing of your book.

Dedication

This is where you thank someone you have deep respect for. It may be your spouse or family or someone who gave you inspiration to write your book. It's up to you.

EDITING

All authors should get their manuscripts edited by professional editors. Money spent on editing and earnings are definitely connected. The more money authors spend on editing, the more earnings they have from their books.

First determine what kind of editing you need.

Proofreading is the cheapest. It looks for basic grammar and spelling errors in your manuscript. Copy editing looks at grammar usage and consistency throughout your manuscript in character descriptions, etc. Line editing puts a higher emphasis on grammar. Substantive editing is the most expensive editing. It can involve deleting, adding or changing the order of entire chapters.

While not all the publishing recommendations in this book offer editing services, many printers and publishers do and their services can often be purchased without getting your book printed there.

Other companies also offer editing services, such as Self Publishing Review. **www.selfpublishingreview.com**

Their rates are one cent per word for proofreading (spelling and grammar) and two cents per word for content editing. Content editing provides notes on character, plot and development of the book. A summary is provided of the issues and merits of the book.

If you don't have the money for editing, I have three suggestions.

You can try **www.autocrit.com/editing/free-wizard/** for fiction books. For $29.97 per month, you can use their editing software. You can cancel anytime. Their software produces a report recommending changes to your manuscript. If you report a problem you're having within 14 days, they'll solve it or give you a refund. They state 58,932 self and traditionally published authors have used their software, many of whom rely on it.

AutoCrit is not a spelling or grammar checker, but it does provide step-by-step recommendations in more than 25 areas for improving your fiction manuscript.

If your manuscript isn't fiction or you also want spelling and grammar checks, try **www.grammarly.com**. They not only check spelling but will even highlight words spelled correctly but used in the wrong context.

You can also try **www.prowritingaid.com**. They provide 20 different reports highlighting changes to make to your manuscript.

COVER DESIGN

Cover design for your book is crucial.

On many websites, people just see your book cover and you have just a few seconds for a potential buyer to decide whether to click on it or not. That's especially true for ebooks.

Likewise in bookstores, a good cover can mean the difference between a potential buyer picking up your book and reading the back cover or just looking elsewhere.

Cover design includes your front cover as well as text for your back cover, except for ebooks where only the front cover is used.

All the recommendations in this book include professional cover design.

New authors shouldn't think they can do it themselves with some cover design template.

Nothing can replace professional cover design.

PAGE LAYOUT

Professional page layout is also strongly recommended.

Some printers now provide authors with information on how to layout the pages of their book.

I recommend you don't do that. Instead use your printer's professional page layout service. It's usually included in any package you purchase.

All the recommendations in this book include professional page layout.

KEYWORDS

Most printers now ask authors to submit keyword searches when they submit their files for publication.

Keywords are words people search for on Amazon looking for a book.

If you can find good keywords, your book will be among the books they see after their search.

You can get keywords from Amazon or Google.

My favorite, however, is **www.kwfinder.com**

KWFinder allows two free searches in 24 hours. If you register with them (no credit card needed), you get five free searches in 24 hours. If you want more, you can get 100 searches a day for $29.08 per month.

Over several days I can do all the searches I need for free.

The key category in the results you get is "search." This will tell you the average monthly search volume in the last 12 months. In other words, how popular is that keyword.

Try to think of keywords other people, not the author, would search for and see how they might match your book.

If you need assistance and want to use Google and Amazon, BookBaby offers a free guide entitled *Unlock Your Amazon Keywords* which can be obtained at **www.bookbaby.com**

CHAPTER

2

A Comment on POD Services

Since the theme of this book is inexpensive books and ebooks, I think I should say something about print-on-demand (POD) companies.

POD technology allows for the printing of just one copy of a book. But printing in such small quantities is expensive, and POD companies mark up their prices.

This results in a higher retail price for a book.

They also take a portion of an author's royalties.

That can result in an even higher retail price.

POD companies will provide you with author copies of your book for a fee, often a large fee. The larger that fee the lower your royalties will be, again forcing you to raise your retail price.

Before long, the high retail price makes it difficult to sell a book that may be priced out of the market.

These companies will also print a book anytime they get an order and send it to the buyer, bookstore or website that ordered it.

While you still have to market your book, it is nice to have a company handle both the print-on-demand side of things and the payment of royalties to you.

But the large POD companies print anything presented to them, except for the obvious offensive stuff.

The result is the vast majority of the books they print sell just a few hundred copies.

So to make their business model work, they often offer discounted or sale prices trying to attract authors to print their book at prices most publishing companies cannot match.

Once you've paid that, they have no incentive to promote your book since it probably won't sell more than a few hundred copies anyway.

Royalty payments are low after the inflated production cost is deducted from your retail price.

Large POD companies will pressure you to buy expensive marketing packages that won't help promote your book.

Every book needs an individual marketing strategy designed for it, specifically appealing to the audience for that title.

Marketing strategies offered by many POD companies are one-size-fits-all and won't reach the specific audience your book requires.

On top of that, libraries and bookstores often won't carry POD titles because they view them as inferior to titles from publishing companies.

Large POD companies are printers, they are not self publishers. They provide an inferior book based on their financial constraints when compared to the quality book produced by actual self-publishing companies.

These printers also won't return the original production files to the author when asked. Why? Because it would make it too easy for authors to go elsewhere.

Many publishers will return the production files to an author. After all, if you paid for them you should own them.

Those publishers include BookLocker, Dog Ear Publishing, Mill City Press, Outskirts Press, Publish Green and Wasteland Press.

Check out the website:
www.wbjbradio.com/viewshow.php?id=42&aid

The website says: "Anyone thinking of publishing a book should go no further without listening to these interviews" on POD printers.

I highly recommend the sixth edition of Mark Levine's book, *The Fine Print of Self-Publishing, A primer on contracts, printing costs, royalties, distribution, ebooks and marketing.*

I especially urge you to read Chapter 8 of his book, where he determines the exact exorbitant markups some POD printers charge their customers.

To sell books today, authors have to make a large commitment to market and promote their work.

If you are not willing to do that, large POD printers may be the answer for you.

But keep in mind, you likely won't sell many books.

Some POD companies are better than others.

BookBaby allows you to sell your book or ebook at whatever price you choose (although for color books there is a minimum price). You'll just get a lower royalty if you price it too low. And they don't pester you to buy their marketing plans.

A few smaller POD companies could be classified as better as well.

I also urge you to read Chapter 9 of Levine's book, where he personally experiences the do-it-yourself (DIY) publishers, namely CreateSpace, IngramSpark and Smashwords.

If you use the DIY options—and you're tech savvy enough to do so—it will be cheaper to get a book and ebook.

But the level of frustration and the likelihood of getting an inferior book cover compared with what a professional cover designer would provide suggests to me you shouldn't DIY.

3

U.S. Book Publishers

PLEASE NOTE: The package prices and other costs charged by the printers and publishers cited in this chapter were compiled in the fall of 2017. If you are interested in purchasing services from any of the companies listed here, please contact them to confirm their current prices.

Author Solutions This company has relationships with leading printers and media companies which they claim gives authors a greater range of publishing and marketing options.

They have relationships in the United States with Archway Publishing, Author House, Balboa Press, iUniverse, LifeRich Publishing, Trafford, WestBow Press and Xlibris.

All of these printers are located in Bloomington, Indiana, as is Author Solutions.

Author Solutions also has several international printing partners.

Author Solutions was purchased by Penguin Books in 2012.[1] In late 2015, Penguin Random House sold Author Solutions to an affiliate of the Najafi Companies, a private investment firm.[2] **www.authorsolutions.com**

Let's look at these U.S. printers individually. All of them are POD printers.

Archway Publishing This printer is a creation of Simon and Schuster and Author Solutions.

Archway is a POD printer with B&W packages for fiction and nonfiction books priced at $1,999, $3,999, $5,299, $9,399 and $13,999. Color packages cost $2,499, $4,399 and $5,499. Children's book packages sell for $1,699, $4,199, $5,299 and $8,399. Business packages go for $2,199, $4,799, $7,299 and $16,999.

None of the packages include an author website.
www.archwaypublishing.com

Author House Another POD service.

B&W packages sell for $899, $1,299, $1,999, $2,899, $5,599, $8,299 and $12,299. The last four offer an author website.

Color packages cost $899, $1,299, $1,999 and $2,899. Children's book packages go for $899, $2,599, $3,999 and $5,999.

None of these offer an author website.
www.authorhouse.com

Balboa Press This POD company, a division of Hay House Inc. in partnership with Author Solutions, specializes in self-help books that aspire to make positive impacts on the world.

Their B&W packages sell for $1,099, $1,899, $2,799, $3,999, $5,599, $8,799 and $14,999. The last five include an author website.

Color packages go for $1,399, $2,099, $3,499, $4,899 and $8,299. None of them offer an author website.

An author website costs $599 or $999 with hosting for one year. After that you pay a renewal fee
www.balboapress.com

iUniverse Another POD service.

B&W packages sell for $999, $1,699, $2,299, $2,999, $4,899, $6,299 and $7,699. Color packages cost $1,499, $2,799 and $5,499.

An author website is offered with the two most expensive packages in both the B&W and color categories. **www.iuniverse.com**

LifeRich Publishing This POD printer is affiliated with Reader's Digest in partnership with Author Solutions.

Fiction packages sell for $1,099, $1,899, $3,299, $4,999 and $8,499. Nonfiction packages cost $1,099, $1,899, $3,299, $5,999 and $9,999. Children's packages go for $1,099, $2,999, $4,999 and $8,399. Finally, cookbook packages sell for $1,099, $1,899, $3,299, $5,399 and $9,999.

None of the packages offer an author website. **www.liferichpublishing.com**

Trafford Publishing A POD service.

B&W and color packages sell for $699, $1,499, $2,499, $3,599, $5,799, $7,999 and $10,999. Children's book packages cost $999, $1,499 and $1,999.

The five most expensive B&W and color packages offer an author website. **www.trafford.com**

WestBow Press POD for Christian authors.

Their Christian B&W publishing packages are priced at $1,099, $1,995, $3,299, $4,399, $6,999 and $16,999. An author website comes with the three most expensive packages. Color packages for children's books and cookbooks, etc. cost $1,799, $3,299 and $6,499.

Independent bookstore stocking of your book costs $5,999 and adding a signing package at the same store costs $7,499. **www.westbowpress.com**

Xlibris "Created by authors for authors" is their marketing slogan.

Xlibris offers POD B&W and color packages for $899, $1,499, $2,099, $3,999, $7,799 and $15,299. An author website is included with the four most expensive packages in B&W.

Specialty packages are offered for Christian books (B&W and color $1,099 and $2,399), poetry (B&W and color $899 and $1,299), children (B&W and color $2,199, $3,199 and $5,999), sci-fi (B&W and color $899, $1,399 and $2,199) and romance ($1,399).

Local bookstore and library placement of your book costs $4,299 and $6,899 for B&W and color books.

Hollywood movie and television chances sell for $999, $2,999, $3,899 and $16,299.

A website can be purchased for $399, $599 and $999 with one year's hosting. Annual renewal is $99. **www.xlibris.com**

Now let's look at other American printing companies.

Abbott Press This Bloomington, Indiana, printer offers three B&W packages costing $999, $1,799 and $2,999.

All three include an ebook. None of them includes an author website.

They don't print books with color interior pages.

An author website costs $399, $599 or $999.

Print royalties are 25% of the retail price in their bookstore and 10% through other stores and websites.

Editing and video services are offered. Hollywood chances cost $1,099, $4,399 and $17,999.
www.abbottpress.com

Blurb This is a DIY book and ebook service.

Design books using their DIY creation tools.

They provide free ISBNs if you use their book creation tools or you can use your own.

You need to be savvy with these tools to design books. You may also get books with inferior covers and page layout compared with what professionals can do.

Blurb also offers several "experts" who will do page layout, cover design or make your whole book for a fee.

Blurb provides printing, either for a specific number of copies or for distribution.

You can choose warehousing and fulfillment or distribution through the Blurb bookstore and through Ingram's over 39,000 bookstores, including Amazon.
www.blurb.com

BookBaby This printer, located in Pennsauken, New Jersey, offers both printed books and POD services.

Watch for their $999 special if your book is 101 to 150 pages. You get a paperback, ebook, worldwide POD distribution of both, 25 free copies along with cover design, interior layout and cover design for your ebook too. That package usually costs $1,600.

BookBaby doesn't otherwise offer packages. They offer a quotation tool where you can add services and obtain the cost.

Authors can create their own website and hosting arrangements at **www.hostbaby.com** or use BookShop, a free service.

BookShop allows authors to use it as a website with BookBaby filling any orders. Authors can also add Amazon,

Barnes & Noble or any of their favorite sites to the page to allow buyers to purchase their book there.

Authors make royalties of 85% on ebook sales when purchases are made through BookBaby via BookShop.

All printers and publishers will add an author's book to their bookstore. But the higher royalties, the use of Book-Shop as your website and the option to add other sites makes BookBaby's BookShop an added feature. **www.bookbaby.com**

BookLocker A DIY and POD printer located in Bradenton, Florida.

BookLocker offers a B&W package for $875 that gets you a book usually in one month. Expedited service within two weeks costs $1,199.

A B&W paperback/hardcover combo adds $499.

A color paperback costs $875; a hardcover color book $975. You have to add interior formatting design fees to both.

A DIY package costs $25 with several services offered as add-ons.

There is an $18 annual fee to keep your book in POD distribution.

Print royalties are 35% of list price when sold from the publisher's website and 15% of list price from other retailers.

BookLocker does not offer an author website.

They don't have a phone number. You must access them through email. **www.booklocker.com**

Book1One This book printer requires PDF submissions.

The Rochester, New York company prints B&W and color books in five business days for softcover, plastic-coil bound and saddle-stitch bound books; 10 business days for hardcover books.

Rush production is available.

They will print quantities of one to 1,000 books.

They offer software to produce photo books.

No marketing or distribution is offered.

www.book1one.com

BookPrinting.com This printer is located in Minneapolis, Minnesota.

They offer the following services, all of them with starting prices (meaning they go up from there):

Cover design $499, interior layout $399, distribution $1,499, editing two cents per word, marketing $499 and an author website $699.

Distribution is through their warehouse. The author pays the shipping cost of sending books from the printer to the warehouse, which are not in the same location.

Royalties on a $15 book through expanded distribution to an online retailer or brick-and-mortar bookstore is $1.63 minus the cost of shipping from the publisher's warehouse to a third-party warehouse (which ranges from 40 cents to $1.50), so your royalty could be as little as 13 cents.

Royalties on a direct-to-consumer sale of a $15 book are $7.70.

They do not have a toll-free telephone number.

www.bookprinting.com

CreateSpace This is Amazon's online printing service. It's a POD printer, located in North Charleston, South Carolina, that offers a cover creator, image gallery and interior reviewer.

They have submission specifications. Those who are not tech savvy may find their specifications frustrating to meet.

Cover PDF support costs $99, a custom cover $399, copy editing $160 (up to 10,000 words), simple interior $249 and custom interior $349.

Their royalty payments on a 184-page book selling for $8.99 is $2.34.

CreateSpace does not offer an author website.

They do not have a phone number. Online assistance is offered. **www.createspace.com**

Dog Ear Publishing This printer is located in Indianapolis, Indiana.

Their B&W and color packages cost $1,599, $2,599, $3,299, $4,299, $5,899 and $8,499.

The four most expensive packages include an author website.

Otherwise, author websites cost $343, $495 or $695.

Editing and marketing options are available.

Dog Ear uses Adobe fonts in the production of their books. Those fonts are not compatible with Microsoft Word fonts. If you want the same fonts in your book as in your Word manuscript, they will attempt to find a similar Adobe font.

They ask that you check your proofs carefully to be sure they match your manuscript words.

You should always check your proofs, but this is an added unnecessary chore. **www.dogearpublishing.net**

Entrada Publishing Entrada is known for book reviews (see Chapter 9). But they also accept books to publish.

If they accept a book, they will handle the costs of producing, printing, marketing and distribution of the book and pay the author royalties.

When they review books, Entrada editors look for compelling stories that might be good candidates to publish. If so, they may approach you to publish your book.

They accept query letters and/or chapter samples if you think your book may be accepted.

If they decline to publish a book, they can help you self publish, including ebook design.

Entrada also offers editing, proofreading, marketing and marketing advice. Professional book or ebook cover design costs $99. **www.entradapublishing.com**

48 Hour Books This printer, located in Akron, Ohio, promises to print your book in 48 hours.

They print bound paperback books and hardcover and coil-bound books. Rush and super rush service is available at extra cost.

If you purchase 100 copies of your book they will give you 25 free extra copies.

They offer free inside page and cover templates for those willing to use them.

No marketing or distribution is offered. **www.48hrbooks.com**

IngramSpark This POD service is located in LaVergne, Tennessee.

A cover template generator, file creation guide and IngramSpark guide are available.

They have submission specifications. Those who are not tech savvy may find their specifications frustrating to meet.

No cover design or typesetting services are offered. Lightning Source does their printing.

The print setup fee is $49. Paperback and hardcover books are available.

Global distribution is offered.

IngramSpark does not offer an author website.

They don't have a phone number. Access is through email and online. **www.ingramspark.com**

Inkwater Press This Portland, Oregon, printer offers six book packages.

A B&W paperback costs $999. A color paperback goes for $1,299. The other packages cost $1,999, $2,999, $3,999 and $4,999.

The four most expensive packages offer an author website and an ebook. Hardcover books are available.

An author/book landing page costs $200. A multi-page website goes for $500.

Inkwater Press does not have a toll-free telephone number. **www.inkwater.com**

Lulu This POD service is located in Raleigh, North Carolina.

Lulu offers book templates to authors to create their own book and covers.

If you have them do it, they offer three B&W and three color packages.

B&W packages cost $999, $1,999 and $2,999. Color packages go for $1,199, $2,199 and $3,199.

The most expensive packages in each category offer an author website and a hardcover book.

An author website costs $399, $599 or $999. The annual website renewal fee is $129.

Elite cover design on its own costs $599.

Editing and marketing services are offered, as well as Hollywood chances ($1,199, $4,399 and $18,499).

On their website, Lulu is asked whether all orders of an author's book will look like the proof copy?

Lulu answers that, while they make every effort to maintain quality, there can be slight differences between printing and binding orders. That difference, they add, will not result in a return or refund.

www.lulujr.com allows children to become published authors. **www.lulu.com**

Mill City Press A book and POD printer located in Maitland, Florida.

A fictional, memoirs and general nonfiction POD book plan costs $1,597, book and ebook POD $2,744; business and brand promotion book POD $2,743, book and ebook POD $3,841; and children's and coffee table book POD $2,744, book and ebook POD $4,041.

Expanded print and ebook plans cost $4,291, $5,289 and $5,289 for the three genres.

You can build your own book publishing plan from a list of services and prices.

An author website costs $799.

www.millcitypress.net

Outskirts Press This printer, located in Parker, Colorado, was named #1 in the Self-Publishing Industry by Top Consumer Reviews in 2016. They also donate every year to The Red Cross, Colorado Humanities and Children's Hospital. Every year the author of their Best Book of the Year receives a $1,500 prize.

Outskirts Press offers three B&W book publishing packages costing $899, $1,199 and $1,895. A color books package goes for $1,996.

A fiction book package goes for $5,481, nonfiction $6,180, spiritual $5,034, children's package with author supplied illustrations $5,569, children's package with no supplied art $8,802, Christian $5,034, spiritual $5,034, cookbooks $4,923, and memoirs $6,182.

Outskirts Press does not offer an author website.

www.outskirtspress.com

Scribe This publisher handles complicated book and ebook layouts.

The Philadelphia, Pennsylvania company has earned a reputation for producing high-quality books and ebooks.

"The production of Bibles for print and digital distribution represents some of the most complex, demanding, and important work in publishing," Scribe's website says.

"Scribe's long history of collaboration with many prominent religious organizations, churches, and publishers puts us in a unique position. We develop, manage, and maintain repositories and databases for eight well-known Bible versions.

"In addition to numerous English and Spanish Bibles, Scribe produces original Hebrew, Aramaic, and Greek versions. Many of our employees are multilingual in classical (e.g., Greek, Hebrew, Latin) as well as modern languages (especially Spanish)."

In short, if Scribe can do that, they can handle anything authors throw at them.

Their marketing slogan is: "A modern application of an ancient craft."

The design and typesetting of an uncomplicated novel-sized book costs about $1,000 without editing and about $2,000 if editing and proofreading are included. Those prices include distribution.

Quotes are provided on a case-by-case basis, depending on the complexity of your book and the source files you provide.

Scribe also offers website design and hosting, indexing and manuscript evaluation.

Distribution is a one-time fee of $150.

They don't have a toll-free telephone number.

http://scribenet.com

Standout Books This company is located outside Manchester, England. But I include them because they have a presence in the U.S. market. Their website ends with .com and not **.co.uk** and they quote all prices in U.S. dollars instead of British pounds, giving the illusion they are an American company.

They offer two print packages, one with a paperback and ebook priced at $1,099 and a second featuring a paperback, ebook and author website for $2,099.

An author website costs $999.

Their phone number is an international call from the United States. **www.standoutbooks.com**

Virtual Bookworm This College Station, Texas company offers some inexpensive book packages.

Their B&W paperback packages cost $360, $440, $495, $790, $1,110, $1,390 and $1,950. Hardcover B&W packages go for $430, $495, $650, $950, $1,330, $1,575 and $2,100.

A B&W paperback and hardcover combo costs $590, $685, $825, $1,050, $1,375, $1,650 and $2,225.

Color packages are priced at $625, $700, $900, $1,200, $1,510, $1,690 and $2,095. Hardcover color packages cost $700, $775, $975, $1,275, $1,585, $1,765 and $2,160.

A color paperback and hardcover combo goes for $1,110, $1,175, $1,375, $1,675, $1,985, $2,165 and $2,560.

The three most expensive packages in each category offer bronze, silver or gold marketing packages. These consist of press releases to 200 media outlets, review copies to major reviewers and business cards, bookmarks and post cards. A "personal storefront" (a website) is included free for two years in each marketing package.

These packages cost $400, $700 or $1,300.

Most packages also come with a website.

A website includes a personal domain name and Virtual Bookworm hosting in order to satisfy orders. If ordered separately, a website costs $240 for one year, $340 for two years and $440 for three years with an option to renew.

Professional editing services are offered.

Book trailers cost $900.

Virtual Bookworm charges $20 in maintenance fees annually after two years ($40 annually after two years for the combined paperback and hardcover packages).

Books are distributed to Amazon, Barnes and Noble, Ingram, Baker & Taylor and listed in Books in Print.

Royalties are 50% of net proceeds.

www.virtualbookworm.com

Wasteland Press This Shelbyville, Kentucky, printer also offers some inexpensive book packages.

The B&W packages start with a basic plan for $245, including a 20-to-125-page paperback book, an ISBN number, custom cover, distribution to online retailers, free shipping in the continental U.S. of five free books and a 15% royalty on books sold through Wasteland and online.

The silver plan offers the same for hardcover books and you get two hardcover copies for $295.

The gold package offers the same as the basic plan but has 75 free paperback books, two free reviews, 1,000 press releases sent out, worldwide distribution, a bookseller returns program in the U.S. and increases the royalty to 25% for $650.

The platinum package is the same as the gold plan but has 150 free paperback books, five free reviews, the bookseller returns program in the U.S., U.K. and E.U. and increases the royalty to 30% for $995.

Finally the ultimate package is the same as the platinum plan but has 500 free paperback books and 10 free reviews for $1,995.

The color basic plan includes two free paperback books and a 10% royalty for $295, the silver plan offers two free hardcover books and 10% royalty for $345, the gold plan features 25 free paperback books and increases the royalty to 20% at a cost of $650, and the platinum plan offers 50 free paperback books and a 25% royalty for $950.

The color plans are limited to 20-to-40-page books. The price is higher for larger books.

Only the $950 color plan offers 1,000 press releases sent out and two free reviews. None of the color plans offers a bookseller returns program. All of the color plans offer online distribution.

They do not offer an author website. They recommend authors set up a page for their book on Facebook.

They don't have a toll-free telephone number, but they have a toll-free fax number. **www.wastelandpress.net**

Xulon Press This Maitland, Florida, printer targets the Christian book market.

Their Christian self-publishing packages cost $999, $1,899, $2,899 and $4,399.

None of these offer an author website. Ebooks are available with the two most expensive packages. **www.xulonpress.com**

CHAPTER
4
Children's Book Publishers

Among the U.S. printers and publishers I cited in Chapter 3, eight offer children's book packages.

The eight are Archway Publishing, Author House, LifeRich Publishing, Mill City Press, Outskirts Press, Trafford Publishing and Westbow Press and Xlibris.

Lulu offers **www.lulujr.com**, which allows children to become published authors.

Many other printers and publishers would maintain that their color packages would accommodate children's books.

CHAPTER

5

The Print Book Winner

PLEASE NOTE: *The prices this publisher charges that are cited in this chapter were compiled in the fall of 2017. If you are interested in purchasing any services from this publisher, please contact them to confirm their current prices.*

And the winner is . . . **Wasteland Press**.
www.wastelandpress.net

This Kentucky publisher allows an author with little money to get their 20-to-125-page B&W paperback book printed and distributed online for only $245, along with a 15% royalty and five free paperback copies with free shipping.

The same page count in a B&W hardcover book is available for $295, including two free copies with free shipping, a 15% royalty and online distribution.

Their gold plan gives an author 75 B&W paperback copies and free shipping (enough for a launch or author signings) for only $650 for the same-sized book. You also get two free reviews and 1,000 press releases sent out, a bookseller returns program in the U.S., a 25% royalty and worldwide distribution.

You can get a 20-to-40-page color paperback book for $295, along with two free paperback books and a 10% royalty. The same-sized color hardcover book is available for

$345, including two free hardcover books and a 10% royalty. For $650 you get a same-page count color paperback book, 25 free books and the royalty increases to 20%.

All three color packages offer online distribution. No bookseller returns program, no press releases are sent out and no press reviews are offered with the $650 color plan. Larger B&W and color books cost more. See their website for details.

All the plans mentioned above offer unlimited reprints of your book.

If you want a book and ebook, the most economical package is at **Virtual Bookworm**.

Their cheapest B&W package costs $360 and an ebook for Amazon, Barnes and Noble, Apple and a PDF to Ingram can be added for $99.

So you get a B&W book and ebook for $459 (add $30 if you have a Contents page). There is an annual $20 maintenance fee after two years. **www.virtualbookworm.com**

CHAPTER

6

In Pursuit of an Ebook

Every author should consider getting an ebook of their book, or even just publishing an ebook.

Ebooks are not expensive (see Chapter 7) and they represent a significant percentage of the book market.

Many readers, including many young readers, just purchase ebooks to read on their devices.

You cannot ignore this market.

Authors should know that their ebook won't look exactly like their printed book.

Ebooks, due to how they flow on e-reading devices and allow the reader to increase type size, don't support page numbers and some tables and graphics.

What price should you charge for your ebook?

Mark Coker, founder of Smashwords, the world's largest distributor of self-published ebooks, wrote the following in his book *The Secrets of Ebook Publishing Success, How to reach more readers with your words*:

"Some (but not all) indie authors who experimented with different price points have reported their book sold more units at $4.99 than at $2.99. Some but not all readers perceive lower cost books as lower quality, and therefore not worth their time. If you're targeting younger readers, they might be more price sensitive than more mature readers. Non-fiction, which is usually purchased to solve a problem or obtain a measureable benefit, can usually support higher prices than fiction."

Coker urges authors to offer their ebooks for free. He admits this works best for authors of several books or a series of novels.

But I disagree with Coker that it is good for an author of a single ebook to sell it for free.

If the ebook has not been selling there's nothing to lose by offering it for free for a limited period of time and then pricing it at $2.99 US and see what happens. Usually you get a bump in sales because word gets around and those who missed the free offer will still buy it for a low price.

Sometimes running a free book promotion will get you the reviews you need to later raise your price and afford to run paid promotions.

But I think offering every single author's first ebook—and possibly only ebook—for free is a mistake. Give it a chance at a low price first.

You sell more ebooks the lower your price. You sell more at 99 cents than at $1.99 or $2.99.

But it depends on your topic and genre. Some nonfiction books can demand a higher price.

Try various prices to see what works for your audience.

Readers are less likely to buy a book with a poor cover and no reviews. That's why I urge authors to pay professionals to design their book covers.

It only makes sense that the more places your book and ebook are located will increase its chances of being found.

This gets me to the debate over KDP Select offered by Amazon. Once enrolled, authors' ebooks can be downloaded free by Amazon Prime members, who are allowed one free download per month. While the author gets paid a royalty for each download, the ebook cannot be available for sale on any other platform, including the author's own website, while it's enrolled in KDP Select.

Amazon demands exclusivity.

I once again refer readers to Coker's book *The Secrets of Ebook Publishing Success, How to reach more readers with your words*. His Chapter 10, or Secret Ten, entitled Avoid Exclusivity, cannot be stressed enough:

"Amazon understands that by capturing hundreds of thousands of exclusive indie books, they'll starve their retail competitors of books to sell, and they'll make these authors more dependent upon Amazon . . .

"In 2012 when Amazon entered India and Brazil, it turned the screws even tighter. Amazon made the 70% royalty option dependent upon your book remaining in the KDP Select program. Otherwise, you only earned 35%."

This demand for exclusivity has resulted in Amazon's market share declining and millions of readers—following their favourite authors—purchasing books from other retailers and reading them on other devices.

"None of the other platforms or retailers push you toward exclusivity," Coker writes. "I think every author should publish at Amazon, but don't enroll in the Select program."

I fully agree with Coker. Avoid the KDP Select program. Smashwords does not offer distribution to Amazon.

Now let's look at ebook producers in the United States. Most of these companies offer cover and interior design in the prices cited. If you already printed your book, you have those services already completed and you may be able to save money, although the inside pages may need some tweeking to meet ebook standards.

BookRix, Draft2Digital, Publish Green and Smashwords produce ebooks, so they were not mentioned in Chapter 3. As a result, I provide their websites after their entries in the list of ebook producers.

PLEASE NOTE: The costs charged by the ebook producers cited in this chapter were compiled in the fall of 2017. If you are interested in purchasing services from

any of the ebook producers listed here, please contact them to confirm their current prices.

Author Solutions companies All the POD companies owned by Author Solutions no longer offer an ebook package. You now have to get a print book to get an ebook.

Blurb Design an ebook using their DIY creation tools.

You can design fixed layout ebooks for a $9.99 conversion fee and no royalty charges from Blurb for Amazon Kindle, Apple iPad, Android devices and Mac or PC computers.

Or design reflowable ebooks for Amazon Kindle and the Apple iBooks store or PDFs costing $4.99 per file that can be shared easily or sold in Blurb's bookstore.

You can also hire their "experts" to design your ebook for a fee.

BookBaby $249 for ebook conversion, $29 for an ISBN, $2 for each image inside your ebook.

BookLocker $199 for simple ebook conversion. Specific criteria must be met to get this price. That price includes already having an ebook cover. Original ebook cover design costs $125.

BookPrinting.com Ebook conversion starts at $299.

BookRix This company offers free ebook production and free distribution to Amazon, Apple iBooks, Kobo and Google Play, as well as through distributor Baker & Taylor.

They pay 70% of net proceeds to authors and provide monthly royalty payments.

They also sell ebooks. Their users can share their writing as well as connect with other readers.

BookRix doesn't have a phone number. They use email to communicate with authors. **www.bookrix.com**

CreateSpace Converts your print-ready book into a Kindle ebook for $79. If not print ready, conversion costs $139.

The ebook will only be available on Amazon Kindle.

Dog Ear Publishing Ebook conversion costs $399.

Draft2Digital This Oklahoma City, Oklahoma company charges no fee to format, make a cover, convert and distribute your ePub ebook.

They take about 10% of the retail price, or 15% of the net proceeds, off every sale as payment.

You can change your price, text or description for free.

You can sell your ebook, even offer it for free everywhere but Amazon, where it will be priced at 99 cents.

But they do have some restrictions on the price you can charge. They only distribute ebooks with minimal pricing based on file size: 99 cents up to 3 MB, $1.99 from 3 MB to 10 MB and $2.99 for files greater than 10 MB.

Draft2Digital says they will supply a print-ready PDF that the author can take to a print-on-demand publisher to get a "pixel-perfect paperback."

ISBNs are free. Preorders up to 90 days can be accommodated, but not on Amazon.

Draft2Digital proudly states they have no stylebook.

They also offer professional cover design, editing, marketing and audio books through several other companies. **www.draft2digital.com**

IngramSpark An ebook setup fee is $25.
The setup fee for a print book and ebook is $49.

Inkwater Press Custom ebook design costs $799.

Lulu An ebook creator guide is available.

Mill City Press An ebook publishing base plan costs $299.
Ebook cover design goes for $249. Rush ebook formatting costs $99.
Ebook distribution costs $99 per year.
A complete ebook plan for fiction, memoirs and general nonfiction ebooks costs $746, business and brand promotion ebooks go for $1,144 and children's and coffee table ebooks cost $1,144.

Outskirts Press An Apple ebook costs $599. An Amazon Kindle ebook and Barnes & Noble Nook ebook each cost $249.
An elite bundle of all three goes for $1,097.

Publish Green Any author with a very complicated print book layout may want to consider Publish Green.
The Maitland, Florida company, which just produces ebooks, offers an enhanced features option that accommodates

drop caps, sidebars, backgrounds and colored text due to their hands-on formatting process.

There are document complexity fees ranging from $50 to $500.

Annual renewal fees for global distribution are $79 and for a personal sales page at **www.mybookorders.com** are $25.

Those fees can make Publish Green rather expensive. But they do good work making ebooks out of complicated print book layouts.

They don't have a toll-free telephone number.
www.publishgreen.com

Scribe An uncomplicated ebook that Scribe has not typeset usually costs between $350 and $500, including distribution.

If Scribe produced the book, the ebook price drops to about $200 or lower.

Smashwords Free ebooks are offered if you can format your manuscript according to their 117-page stylebook.

Smashwords, located in Los Gatos, California, works on commission, meaning they take 15% or less of the net proceeds or 10% of the retail price of your ebook sales.

Ebooks sold on their distribution network earn a royalty of 60% of the list price. An ebook sold in the Smashwords' store earns a royalty of up to 80% of the list price.

Smashwords does not distribute ebooks to Amazon, although they encourage authors to do so.

Distribution is to Apple, Barnes & Noble, Kobo and many other sites.

Authors can create coupons giving readers or reviewers discounts or free ebooks. The coupons can only be used at Smashwords' store.

Smashwords' ebook conversion system is called Meatgrinder.

Smashwords can't make a perfect ebook for you because, they admit, if they did they couldn't offer a free service.

They also admit several attempts may be needed to get Meatgrinder to accept a 117-page stylebook-formatted ebook.

Smashwords does not offer an author website.

They also have no telephone number. Access is by email and online. **www.smashwords.com**

Standout Books An ebook package costs $799.

Virtual Bookworm For $199 for B&W ebooks you get an ebook for Amazon, Barnes and Noble, Apple and a PDF to Ingram. The cost of all these formats for color ebooks and any ebook with over 15 images is $299.

If a POD print package is purchased, the ebook formats cost is reduced to $99 and $150.

They will convert printed copies of your manuscript into ebook format for $2 per page.

An added option allows ebooks to be distributed free of charge to libraries to permit digital loaning.

Wasteland Press With the purchase of a print book package, the cost of a Kindle ebook is $150, an Apple iBook $150 and a Nook ebook $50.

Purchased separately the prices rise to $250, $250 and $150 respectively.

An eSupreme package gives you all three for $500. Free ebook cover design is included.

CHAPTER

7

The Ebook Winners

PLEASE NOTE: *The prices charged by the ebook producers cited in this chapter were compiled in the fall of 2017. If you are interested in purchasing services from these companies, please contact them to confirm their current prices.*

And the winners are . . .

OPTION #1 (FREE EBOOKS)

Draft2Digital in Oklahoma City, Oklahoma.
www.draft2digital.com
They offer free ebooks and free price, description and text changes for 15% off each sale's net proceeds.
But the size of your ebook may restrict the price you can charge (see Chapter 6 for details).

OPTION #2 (PAID FOR EBOOKS)

BookBaby in Pennsauken, New Jersey.
www.bookbaby.com
BookBaby offers ebook conversion for $249.
Buying an ISBN number costs $29. And adding an image to the inside of your ebook costs $2 per image.
Ebook cover design and text formatting cost more.

But if you are bringing your print book to BookBaby, you'll get an ebook for $278 (no images).

Lifetime distribution is included.

For $278 you get:

1   File conversion to an ebook.
2   Graphics conversion.
3   A proof in six to eight business days.
4   Free listings on Goodreads, Book Daily, Noisetrade and Bublish.
5   Free reviews from Reader's Favorite and Story Cartel.
6   Free memberships and discounts at Author Marketing Club, Writer's Cube, Smith Publicity Promotion Services, PR Newswire, Circle of Seven Productions, Riffle, Book Riot and Self-Publishing Review.
7   Free guide on social media tips for authors.
8   Free changes to your pricing, author bio, book description.
9   Global distribution through the largest ebook partner list in the industry.
10 BookShop (see **Chapter 3** for details).
11 High royalties—85% of gross ebook sales from BookShop.
12 Get paid weekly whenever the pay point you set is reached.

BookBaby has been called a handholding service. But I prefer that to the hit and miss of running your potential ebook for the second or third time through the Meatgrinder at Smashwords.

Any author with a very complicated print book layout may want to consider **Publish Green**.
www.publishgreen.com

Scribe also handles complicated book layouts and provides high-quality ebooks.

They produce all ebook formats (ePub, Mobi and PDF), something many ebook producers don't do, including all Author Solutions POD companies. They only produce the nearly universal ePub. **http://scribenet.com**

CHAPTER
8
The Book Launch

It's time to hold your book launch.

First, let's deal with the subject.

Joel Friedlander has written an excellent blog entitled *12 Tips for Successful Book Launch Parties.*

His subheads: "Make a budget, plan a venue, plan your space, get the word out, keep people entertained, make sure you have books, use the media, build your crowd, take pictures, how to sign (books), prizes and giveaways and gather (email) addresses" show how to organize a book launch better than I've seen it anywhere else.

Be sure to look for it at **www.thebookdesigner.com**

A book launch takes time to plan and execute well, especially if it's your first foray into promoting your book. Rental fees, whether to serve food and drinks, arranging promotional material in time such as business cards, postcards and bookmarks. All these have to be considered.

But a book launch is well worth the effort if it successfully gets your book off the ground and you sell a lot of books.

Some printers sell a package promising to tell you how to launch your book. In 2016 Standout Books offered a Book Launch Marketing Plan for $399.

You can do this!

You don't need initial and final "30-minute consultations with a book marketing expert" at Standout Books to make it work.

Follow Friedlander's advice and do it yourself.

I'd also recommend a blog, *6 Ways to Give a Better Book Reading*, at **www.friesenpress.com**

If you're going to read a portion of your book at your book launch or at book readings or book signings, check out this blog to hone your reading skills.

9

Marketing Your Book

PLEASE NOTE: *The prices cited in this chapter were compiled in the fall of 2017. If you are interested in any of these services, please contact that website to confirm their current prices.*

Now that a book launch is behind you, it's time to really promote your book.

Take a moment to get a dose of reality about the publishing industry and marketing your book.

Google the words "10 Awful Truths about Book Publishing" and read Steven Piersanti's 10 points. He's president of Berrett-Koehler Publishers.

After reading that, you'll realize selling your book is primarily up to you.

Before starting to market your book, determine the audience you hope to sell it to. Then you can target your marketing to those possible buyers.

Now let's look at 25 great ways to market your book/ebook. You don't have to do all 25. That's okay. Just select those that you can afford to do.

1. First and foremost, an author website is key to your marketing efforts.

Writer and speaker Jamie Arpin-Ricci has written about the importance of an author website:

"There are many ways to market your book . . . but perhaps the most important is the author website. Having your own website is critical to building your identity as a writer, as well as creating a central connecting point for your readers.

"Even if you rely heavily on social media platforms to promote your work or connect with readers, don't put all your eggs in that basket. Those sites can change (or disappear) with little notice, so your own site can be the constant your 'brand' needs to flourish in the long term."

Go to **www.jamiearpinricci.com** to read the whole article.

Make your website more than just a place to sell your book. Make it informative, even entertaining. Run contests on your website. Be creative.

Write an interesting author bio. Let readers feel they know or can relate to you.

2. Organize an email list of readers who have bought your book. These are your most loyal fans. You can use the list to inform them of any awards you win, contests you run or any new book you have coming.

3. Also important is blogging. Blogging is a very good way to regularly attract people to your thoughts and words and they can be counted on to purchase your present and future books. Blogs provide a platform to attract fans and market and promote your books.

If you decide to blog, BookBaby's free guide *Blogging 101 for the Independent Author* will help you get started. The guide shows you how to develop an audience and market your blog. Go to **www.bookbaby.com**

And remember, if you blog keep to a schedule so your fans know when to search for your latest blog.

Joel Friedlander asks whether fiction authors should blog.

"Do these blogs work in attracting fiction readers? I think that's more problematic. Obviously, they can't hurt, but it seems to me that people read novels for different reasons than they read informational articles."

"I've had this conversation with numerous novelists, and some, like Joanna Penn, who is both a novelist and a very successful blogger, have suggested there are other things that might be better for fiction writers (until they become mega-famous, of course) to focus on when it comes to marketing your books.

"These might include: concentrating on getting the best book cover you can afford for your book; making sure you have killer sales copy for the back cover and everywhere your book will be listed; offering a sample chapter or look inside the book to entice readers into the story; creating a book review program when your book is new; and making sure your book is widely available and attractively priced.

"So if you're a novelist, should you be blogging?" Friedlander asks. "At this point, the answer is 'it depends,' but for the right writer with an appreciative audience, blogging can be a powerful way to create community around your books. Until you get those fans, put all your efforts into writing great books and promoting them as your long-term plan."

Read Friedlander's articles and blogs at **www.thebookdesigner.com** He also writes for **www.createspace.com**

4. Networking your book on social media is important.

Create an author page on Facebook and be active on other social media sites, like Twitter.

If your time is limited, just promote your book and engage with members on Facebook. Facebook has more readers than any other social media site.

5. Get business cards and bookmarks. Yes, bookmarks. Readers love them. Don't get post cards. People don't mail them.

You can get sale cards the size of post cards with your cover on one side and details about your book and where to buy it on the other.

But business cards with your cover on one side can accommodate both these features.

6. Create an author page on **www.goodreads.com** and share your book with their many members. Be sure to create an author page on Amazon.

7. Advance Reading Copies of your book can be sent to reviewers at least two months before your publication date in order to get reviews to include in your book or on the back cover.

The more reviews you can get, even if you can only use a few choice words, can make a big difference.

8. Taking presale orders on Amazon can help build fan support.

9. Personal marketing to people you know and people they know is also important. Lots of authors sell most of their books to friends, family and acquaintances.

Remember holidays when promoting your book. Suggest your book as an ideal Christmas gift or stocking stuffer.

Don't ask your family or close friends to review your book on Amazon. Amazon has a rule against having close relationships with reviewers and it can lead to your book being banned from Amazon.

10. Appearing at trade shows, book fairs, arts festivals and other events can also promote your book and drive sales.

11. Promoting your book in the local media is important if the local media cares about new local authors, which they sometimes don't. Some newspapers review books. If so, seek them out. A nonfiction author can also target beat reporters covering the issue written about. That can sometimes be more effective.

If you find local media that cares about local authors, organize a press kit. Print extra book covers and include a press release about your book.

12. Quotes promoting your book can be important in marketing it.

If you wrote a book about bird watching, contact a well-known bird expert for a short quote.

This can also work for selling books. Books about fishing and other sports should be brought to the attention of sports stores. Curling clubs should be informed about your curling book.

Be creative. Where can you get quotes to market your book?

13. Some books can be targeted to the educational market. Check with school boards.

14. You can try selling your book to libraries. You can also donate your book to libraries for others to access.

If you wrote a nonfiction book, ask libraries if they would like you to speak. Speaking engagements can help you draw attention to your book and cement your image as an expert in your field of writing. You can then build that image into other speaking appearances.

Don't just think of libraries for speaking engagements. Chambers of Commerce, local Rotary clubs, Knights of Columbus. All kinds of groups have monthly meetings and would welcome speakers on a variety of topics.

Libraries are also a great place to set up book readings, giving you the opportunity to read a portion of your book to an audience of possible buyers.

Book readings can be organized in all sorts of places, from retirement homes to churches, locally owned bookstores and schools.

You can also donate your book to day-care facilities, schools and women's shelters.

Do a book reading in the town or city where your book takes place. Donate your book in that community.

15. Be sure to add an email signature to the end of all your emails promoting you as an author and the books you've published. Give readers a reason to go to your book on Amazon or to your website.

16. A significant way to promote your book is to get it reviewed. I don't mean by Amazon readers, although I'm not discounting that promotion. I'm talking about reviews from one of the review services, free or paid. They are great for the back cover or the first page or pages of your book.

Free services include:

Readers' Favorite Book Reviews where a staff of 500 review books submitted to their website. The reviewers are not assigned books to review but choose books they are interested in. This is an attempt to copy the purchases made at a bookstore, their website says. They only post good reviews. In the case of a poor review, private constructive comments are provided to the author. **www.readersfavorite.com**

Story Cartel where people visiting their website can gain access to books for free if they agree to review them later. The books are given to the site by authors seeking reviews from readers. **www.storycartel.com**

Paid review sites include:

Entrada Book Reviews charges $289 for a book review that is completed in five to eight weeks. Rush service costs $389 and takes three to four weeks. Reviews are 250 to 350 words. They don't promise a positive review, but if it's negative the author has 10 days to ask that it not be published. **www.entradapublishing.com**

Kirkus Reviews cost $425 for a 250-word review. Longer 500-word reviews are available for $575. Children's 200-word book reviews cost $350. All reviews take seven to nine weeks. Reviews of two or three books are available for $699 and $999 respectively. Expedited prices are available at their website. Negative reviews can be killed. **www.kirkusreviews.com**

BlueInk Reviews cost $395 and take seven to nine weeks, $495 within four to five weeks, and a two review package including a BlueInk and Foreward Clarion review costs $695. BlueInk reviews are between 250 and 300 words. A Clarion review is regularly priced at $499 and is between 400 and 500 words. Since reviewers prefer hard copies, if you get a double review a $19.95 fee is charged by BlueInk to cover printing costs for those who submit PDFs instead of mailing in books. **www.blueinkreview.com**

17. If you got your book or ebook from BookBaby, you get a valuable marketing option from Self Publishing Review.

In addition to free blogs and 20% off reviews, you also get a free author interview.

A 10-question interview and your book's cover are featured on a unique, permanent webpage for the author to share and promote as he or she likes. It will initially be featured in an interview author picture box on the site's home page which visitors can click to see the whole interview.

Even if you didn't get your book from BookBaby, go to **www.selfpublishingreview.com** for lots of author services.

18. If you win an award, SHOUT IT FROM THE ROOFTOPS!

Feature the award in your email signature, on business cards, on your website, on social media and on online booksellers like Amazon. EVERYWHERE!

Even if you don't win, tell your fans you were nominated or cited by the awards committee.

19. If a reader emails you saying they loved your book, ask them to write an Amazon review.

You can also write at the end of your book an invitation for readers to review your book on Amazon.

Reader reviews are important to selling your book. You can spend a lot of time contacting Amazon Top Reviewers on Amazon's website. But they often get hundreds of requests.

Another way is to go to www.bookreviewtargeter.com and purchase their software that complies with Amazon rules.

Yearly plans cost $97, $147 or $197. I have not used this software, but very successful authors have and trust it.

20. If you write a series of books it's easier to market and promote them. You can give away the first ebook to get readers hooked, then sell them the second and third books or ebooks.

21. Join a local book club or writers' group.

22. If you can afford it, make a video for your book and put it on your website. A cheaper alternative is to make a book trailer.

23. Again, if you can afford it, make an audio book. Don't read your own book! Hire a professional reader.

24. Buy ads on Amazon promoting your book or ebook to their thousands of visitors every day. It's a great way to get sales on a new book or one that hasn't sold any copies for months.

Dave Chesson on his Kindlepreneur website offers a free three-hour course on everything you need to know to set up and use Amazon ads to sell your book. **You set how much you want to spend**. He gets pretty technical at times, but you'll get a good idea how to do it. Go to www.kindlepreneur.com and ask for it.

Or Chesson recommends you let Book Ads+ do it for you.

For $49 per month and a minimum ad budget of $10 a day, they will create 10 ads using their tactics and keyword master lists. They will create new ads to keep your campaign profitable. The whole thing will cost you $359 a month (31 days times $10 plus $49). You can cancel anytime. **www.bookads.co** (that's right .co)

25. Now let's turn to marketing ebooks.

Ebook sales promotions are all the rage on the Internet.

The best place to sell ebooks is on

www.bookbub.com

You are guaranteed to sell ebooks in one of their featured deals. Countless authors have had great success on BookBub.

But it is expensive and they have very strict acceptance criteria you have to meet to get your ebook featured in one of their daily email alerts to readers matching your genre.

The high standards include lots of reader reviews and a great cover.

You likely won't be accepted, but try it anyway.

They claim the most expensive genre—crime—sells an average of 3,160 ebooks in a featured deal.

If you are accepted, they claim a featured ebook deal will increase your earnings by 196 per cent.

If you don't get a deal on Bookbub, you can try **www.bargainbooksy.com** or **www.bookdaily.com** for more reasonably priced ebook sales promotions.

Bargainbooksy consists of four different promotions.

At **www.bargainbooksy.com**, a promo costs $25 to $150 depending on your genre for an email blast to their 277,000 registered readers.

At **www.freebooksy.com**, a promo costs $40 to $200 depending on your genre sent to their 368,000 readers.

At **www.redfeatherromance.com**, a free ebook promo costs $125, an ebook priced between 99 cents and $1.99 costs $80 and an ebook priced at $2.99 or more costs $100. You must meet some editorial guidelines to get this promo.

At **www.newinbooks.com**, their book launch promo package costs between $299 and $499 depending on your genre.

At **www.bookdaily.com**, they charge $49 a month for several email blasts to their 50,000 readers. A free ebook download deal costs $50 for 300 clicks to your Amazon sales page.

There are also many free ebook promotion websites. One of the best is **www.awesomegang.com**

You can also go once again to Dave Chesson's Kindlepreneur website. He offers, free of charge, a long list of free and paid ebook promotion websites. He also offers a free PDF outlining his best ebook promo sites. **www.kindlepreneur.com**

Running these promotions between Thanksgiving and Christmas is a great idea. If you regularly send emails to your fans, this is a good time to do it.

CHAPTER
10
Options for Novelists

PLEASE NOTE: *The package prices and other costs charged by the publishers cited in this chapter were compiled in the fall of 2017. If you are interested in purchasing services from any of the publishers listed here, please contact them to confirm their current prices.*

So you've finished writing the great American novel and want to get it printed and into ebook format.

I offer four options for novelists.

OPTION #1

Wasteland Press (**www.wastelandpress.net**) offers their gold plan for a 300-page book for $1,100.

You get 75 paperback books (with free shipping in the continental U.S.), just right for a book launch and author signings, two book reviews and 1,000 press releases sent out, a booksellers return program in the U.S., a 25% royalty and worldwide POD distribution.

If you want an ebook, for $350 you'll get all the Kindle, Nook and iBooks formats and full distribution.

Add a hardcover version of your book for $250.

If you need more books you can order author copies.

So for $1,700 you'd have a paperback, hardcover and three ebook formats, as well as full POD distribution and some marketing assistance.

Wasteland Press does not offer a website. In Chapter 8, I told you how important I think it is for an author, especially a novelist, to have a website.

This book is devoted to finding inexpensive solutions for authors.

In keeping with the theme of this book, I would suggest our novelist create a website at **www.wix.com**, **www.squarespace.com** or **www.weebly.com**. These are the easiest website builders for people with very little technical knowledge of coding and other complexities.

For that reason, I don't recommend **www.wordpress.com**, which is not easy to learn for beginners.

Novelists can also pay one of many website creation services that are available on the Internet to get their website produced for them.

I also urge authors use PayPal on their websites.

It is the cheapest, most efficient way to sell books to your fans.

OPTION #2

The following two publishers do not meet the theme of this book regarding inexpensive options for authors. That's why they are not listed in Chapter 3.

But to help novelists, I thought if they don't wish to follow Option #1, I should offer other options if they have the resources to accept them.

The first such publisher is **Wheatmark Publishing** in Tucson, Arizona. **www.wheatmark.com**

Wheatmark doesn't offer packages. They issue custom proposals starting at $2,500.

The cost of a typical publishing project is between $5,000 and $7,000. That includes editing, publishing, print and selling books and ebooks. They also offer ghostwriters.

Royalties are 25% of net print sales and 50% of net ebook sales.

Their website says that since 2000, they have published more than 1,700 titles, including "nearly 100 clients who've sold at least 2,000 copies of their books. Some have gone on to sell 5,000, 10,000 or 25,000 copies, license their translation or movie rights, and even land traditional publishing deals."

Wheatmark can also help you find an agent to land a traditional deal or help you start your own publishing company.

Their marketing is through Authors Academy, which charges $37 a month for membership. They also create websites and blogs.

They begin with a 30-minute complimentary publishing consultation over the phone.

After that, a book publishing blueprint and a book marketing blueprint cost $97 each. Both go for $147. These outline their plans for your book and how to market it, targeting your specific genre.

If you like what they offer, you can continue with the blueprint charges going toward your publishing costs. If you are not satisfied, you can get a complete refund.

OPTION #3

The other publisher that wasn't in **Chapter 3** is **Dorrance Publishing** in Pittsburgh, Pennsylvania.
www.dorrancepublishing.com

Dorrance has been in business since 1920 and it shows.

First-time author: No problem.

The testimonials on Dorrance's website show they have developed handholding into an art form.

Your book is a mess but you want to publish it: No problem.

Dorrance has experienced editors, writing coaches and ghostwriters who listen to what the author wants in their book.

Many authors in the testimonials are first-time authors who speak glowingly of their experience at Dorrance.

In addition to editing, Dorrance provides layout, cover design, publishing and marketing assistance.

After you submit your manuscript, they read it and provide you with a custom publishing proposal offering services and production options based on your goals and your book.

They will submit your book for copyright registration and obtain a Library of Congress Control Number (if your book is eligible) as well as an ISBN and barcode.

Each Dorrance proposal includes a $1,000 promotion and marketing campaign tailored specifically to your book.

They compile a review and publicity list and submit a press release to about 300 media contacts as well as online news media and RSS news feeds, appropriate for the book.

Dorrance takes input from the author, allowing him/her to supply 10 media or book publishing contacts and supplying printed review copies to them.

They send 100 color direct marketing post cards to the author for personal use and spend $200 on Google ads, including keywords. A limited preview is sent to Google Books.

Dorrance creates a New Book Project Summary, a full color marketing release introducing the book, and sends it to 25 selected booksellers and 10 libraries in the author's area.

They'll also call up to 12 selected booksellers in that area trying to arrange autograph sessions.

Dorrance distributes book release data to up to 20 wholesalers, distributors, jobbers and major book chains announcing availability of the book.

The book is distributed to Ingram's Lightning Source and to Baker & Taylor for faster international distribution and bookstore availability.

They submit the book to **Amazon.com** and Barnes and Noble, to the Dorrance bookstore (**www.dorrancebookstore.com**) and to Books in Print, an essential source for booksellers and libraries.

They include the book in their monthly newsletter that goes to tens of thousands of people.

Dorrance also enters the book in their Press Room where media can access the book's details and order copies for review.

Their POD process allows anyone ordering your book or ebook to get prompt service. They also provide a toll-free number for customer questions.

This is potentially the most effective marketing effort offered by any self-publishing company.

They provide several additional marketing options, from an ad in the *New York Times Book Review* costing $3,400 to an audio book package costing $40 per page.

Book trailers cost $549, $2,499 and $4,449. Mini-movie and animation book trailers are also available.

A three-page website, with hosting for one year, costs $499.

I submitted this book to Dorrance and asked for a print book and ebook. The proposal they provided quoted a total cost of $4,900, including $1,000 for marketing. That also included 25 paperback books sent free of charge to the author.

If I paid the total cost during the month I contacted them, the price was lowered to $3,900. If I declined editing, which was called for in the proposal (my book had already been edited), the price dropped to $3,150.

That price would be much higher for a novelist's book.

OPTION #4

Dorrance Publishing has a lower-cost alternative, **RoseDog Books**.

RoseDog offers B&W and color packages costing $980 and $1,980. Both include a paperback book and ebook and distribution.

About $1,000 in marketing assistance is offered in the $1,980 package.

Three free author copies are provided. More can be purchased.

B&W book illustrations cost $100 each, color book illustrations $150 each

Hardcover books are available.

Contact Dorrance Publishing (**www.dorrancepublishing.com**) for more details.

Readers' Favorite offers lots of options for novelists.

Proofreading, editing and manuscript critique services are offered for a fee.

Dozens of free articles are available on their website to help authors find a literary agent.

They also offer reviews and a press release to 800 news, television and radio outlets (see website for costs).

You can use the free press release to promote your book if you don't want to pay for the media outlets. You have to get a favourable review of your book by Readers' Favorite to get the press release, but the review is free unless you want it faster.

Readers' Favorite says sending the press release is unlikely to result in you getting a call about your book. The news outlets will add your press release to their news feeds and Google will index them.

Google's indexing will raise the Google ranking of your book, your Amazon page and your review page on Reader's Favorite.

If you have your website and social media pages on your review page, their Google ranking should also increase.

Go to **www.readersfavorite.com** for more details.

CHAPTER

11

My Final Recommendation

My final recommendation won't be appreciated by printers and publishers, but will be by first-time authors and, especially, authors who had a bad experience publishing their first book.

Once you decide which printer you want to bring your manuscript to readers, Google the company's name.

If you find *A LOT* of complaints about that company, you might want to pause.

That's not to say that lots of authors don't get pristine books from that printer and have a great experience. But *A LOT* of complaints increases your odds of having a bad experience.

If the complaining authors had their issues resolved, then those cases shouldn't reflect on the company. But if they weren't resolved after several attempts and the authors paid for the work done and left in disgust, that's another matter.

If you choose a company to print your book that has faced many complaints, ask them about those complaints and how they were resolved before you pay a cent.

These companies should be accountable to authors.

NOTES

CHAPTER 3

1   Jim Milliot, *Author Solutions Sold to Private Equity Firm*, January 5, 2016. **www.publishersweekly.com**
2   Ibid.

ABOUT THE AUTHOR

Born and raised in Hamilton, Ontario, Canada, William Allan graduated with a Bachelor of Arts degree from McMaster University and a Bachelor of Journalism degree from Carleton University's School of Journalism.

He moved west and started a career with newspapers that lasted nearly 30 years. Most of that time was spent at *The Leader-Post*, the daily newspaper in Regina, Saskatchewan.

He retired in 2008 and lives with the love of his life Abby Ulmer and their cat Toby in Regina.

In 2016, William self published his first book, *Four Murders in a Small Town*, a short fictional crime story.

He followed that up in late 2016 with *How to Self Publish Inexpensive Books and Ebooks*, which he wrote after his trial and error ordeal getting his first book printed. He wanted to help first-time authors avoid that and help them choose a publisher and sell their books. He also researched the many printers and publishers in order to expand his second book beyond just his own experience.

In early 2018, William self published *Justice Preserved*, a collection of 12 fictional crime stories.

He also wrote and published, in spring 2018, a fully updated U.S. edition of his second book to try to help American first-time authors get published.

Will William write and publish more books?

"Living on a fixed income, it would be a challenge to publish another book," he said recently. "We won't be taking a vacation in 2018 so I can publish my third and fourth books. I'm using my royalties from my first two books to help pay the cost of my two 2018 books."

William's book publishing future is unclear.

If this is his final book, first-time authors should be glad he devoted his last book to them and their success. And William couldn't have written a better book, earning a five-star review for his final effort.

OTHER BOOKS BY
WILLIAM ALLAN

The Canadian first edition of this book, *How to Self Publish Inexpensive Books and Ebooks*, listing both Canadian and U.S. publishers, is available at
www.howtoselfpublish.ca

The ebook can be purchased at your favorite online bookseller.

AN EXCERPT FROM WILLIAM ALLAN'S NEW BOOK *JUSTICE PRESERVED*, AVAILABLE NOW.

The next day, (Private Detective Frank) Johnson walked to his front door on the way to lunch with Inspector Bob Nelson.

He opened the door and was met by a man who pushed him back into his home and drew a handgun.

The man wore dark pants and a black coat. He looked like the boy next door, clean shaven, a very handsome man.

But that handsome man was pointing a gun at Johnson.

"You've stuck your nose into something you shouldn't have," the man said. "You won't again."

The man slowly pulled the trigger.

Johnson closed his eyes, waiting to die.

Johnson faces death several times in *Justice Preserved*.

Each time you ask: How will he get out of this one? Will he?

Justice Preserved introduces Private Detective Frank Johnson and Police Inspector Bob Nelson to readers. The book offers 12 crime stories, the Top 12 cases in Johnson's long career.

PRAISE FOR *JUSTICE PRESERVED*

The detective is "harking back to a kind of Sherlock Holmes but updated to the modern era—performing in a series of suspenseful vignettes . . ."
"Some unique thoughts taken for chapter plots."
"Intriguing" stories.
"The writing is concise, sparse, and frequently hard hitting, precisely what is required of most detective fiction."
Joel R. Dennstedt for Readers' Favorite

"This is an interesting, noir-ish concept . . .
"They're both brave men of action . . .
"The author writes dialog and action very well . . ."
Entrada Book Reviews

JUSTICE PRESERVED IS AVAILABLE NOW AT YOUR FAVORITE ONLINE BOOKSELLER.

AND FINALLY . . .

If you found this book helpful, I'd really appreciate a review on Amazon.

No matter how short, reviews have an impact on how a book sells.

Each review will help get this book into the hands of new first-time authors, which I hope we can agree would be a good thing.

Thanks.
William Allan